Copyright by ABC Global Investments, INC

I0503868

Formulas courtesy of:

Yahoo/Finance   **Finviz.com**

Reproduction or translation of any part of this work without the permission of the copyright owner is unlawful. Any request for permission to reproduce any part of this work should be addressed to ABC global Investments, Inc.

Any trade or examples herein is for educational purpose only. While it is believed that the techniques used herein to select stocks are effective, no guarantee as to the success of these techniques is written or implied.

There is no guarantee in this book regarding any investment, written or implied. Individual results may vary substantially from those illustrated in this book.

Contents: Pages

Preface --3 - 4

Chapter 1   General --------------------------------5 - 12

Chapter 2   Objectives----------------------------13 - 17

Chapter 3   Financial Conditions----------------18 - 25

Chapter 4   Profit and Loss-Personal-----------26 - 29

Chapter 5   Adjustments---------------------------30 - 32

Chapter 6   Fearless Investment-----------------33 - 35

Chapter 7   Fundamentals and Technical's----36 - 46

Chapter 8   Identified Lists------------------------47 - 64

Chapter 9   Investment----------------------------65 - 69

Chapter 10 Follow Up------------------------------70 - 77

Chapter 11 Goals------------------------------------78 - 81

Chapter 12 New Balance Sheet------------------82 - 86

Chapter 13 Defense Mechanism----------------87 - 90

Chapter 14 Final Summary-----------------------91 - 97

Preface:

I wanted to write this book to summarize my experience of 35 + years in the stock market. This is a great wealth building exercise if done with utmost discipline.

It requires a long range strategy and dedication to the market, and realizing forces behind the market. If the tools are used with discipline and faith, it can bring in desired results beyond imagination. This is applicable to stock market anywhere in world.

Set up your goals, targets and compare to see if they are achieved in your time frame. If not, be ready to adapt to change and success will follow you. First of all, have faith in self and set up goals and then follow the planned strategy. Investment is following mass psychology ahead of time.

I wanted to dedicate this book to my wife, Rebecca, who has believed in me always, stood by with me, and has faith in me that I can achieve whatever I dream.

Chapter 1: GENERAL:

Objectives:

Before deciding to invest in stocks, think and write down your financial objectives, goals. Remember this book is written for investments in common stocks only to help you achieve goals. This strategy can be applicable in **any global stock market**. Stocks anywhere in world follow the same mass psychology.

Why do you need to set up goals and objectives first? I personally think that this will help you understand better as to which strategy to follow, to achieve it.

Goals need to be set up in the horizon of short and long term.

Short term can be for one year and long term can be for 5 to 10 years and beyond. Why we need long term planning because we are never always right. However stock market has never failed to reach a new high in the long run. Hence our chances of achieving success in long run are much higher. Be realistic in setting up goals. But if we follow path with discipline, we can achieve more than what we planned. In next chapter we will discuss about setting up goals, targets.

Financial Conditions:

Before deciding to invest into stock market, one should sit down and write down their personal financial situation. I myself am a CPA and hence believe in preparing a personal balance sheet first. Write down what assets do you have including all liquid assets and non liquid assets and what are your liabilities, both short term and long term. The main objective to invest in stock market , eventually is to make us completely debt free life and planned balance sheet will have assets only with very little or no liabilities whatsoever. In next chapter we will show format of personal balance sheet/financial statement to prepare.

Profit and Loss –personal:

Again, being CPA, I would suggest preparing personal profit and loss account periodically to see that are you ahead of your planned targets. In other chapter, I will give a simple format of personal profit and loss accounting, which I would suggest to updating every year. Remember to set up goals and targets first and compare with prepared financials at the end of the year to assess total progess.

Adjustments:

If we do not achieve our planned targets, we must be flexible enough to change the strategy and sector changes, acceptance of the facts that where we went wrong and be ready to re-plan investments as per the directions of market. I will discuss this in other chapters.

Fearless Investment:

Investments in stocks should be done without fear but with faith in the system and in the companies identified, discussed in other chapters. One must study basic fundamentals of the company identified first, followed by technical's and market conditions

Fundamentals and Technical's:

Fundamentals of underlying companies are most important and criteria's are discussed in other chapters. Without strong fundamentals of a company, it may not help in long run.

This should be followed by technical's which is also discussed in other chapters

Identified List:

Once the list of identified companies is ready, we can follow the process of short listing of companies and be ready as discussed herein separately. The identification of companies as per given guidelines should be done on regular basis as more may come under the radar. Criteria's are discussed to identify companies to invest separately.

Investment:

Now it is time to Invest out of short listed investment list. We have discussed in separate chapter percentage allocation and timing, averaging etc to deploy available funds.

Follow Up:

We should follow up and evaluate our investments done based on above and see that they perform as per our goals periodically. We need to do this exercise frequently and adjust it as required. We have also discussed this in separate chapters

Goals:

If we set up reasonable goals and follow the path, they can be achieved over a period of time. Allow to set long term goals to have financial freedom from all debts

New balance sheet:

At the end of the year prepare personal balance sheet/financial statement as per the format and compare to see they are improving on asset side compared to last year and moving towards our targets.

Defense Mechanism:

Defense mechanism is general safety points which will help guide thru the process and give us confidence to deploy formulas.

Final Summary:

A simplified summary needs to be made so that we are ready with easy format of formulas and strategy. Always keep handy formulas, percentages & guarding poings.

Now let me discuss each and every chapter as above in details.

Chapter 2: Objectives:

Objectives of investment in stock market along with the goals are most important first step. Why do we decide to invest in stocks? We must have clarity. The objectives are

A. To have financial freedom and debt free life
B. Solid and strong retirement funds
C. Have reasonable wealth for self and family
D. Have some additional continuity of income

The best way to define objectives is to sit down and write all parameters and set up goals and targets. Targets have to be reasonable and achievable. There are various aspects to consider

A. How much liquidity one has available to invest in stock market
B. What is short term and long term investment returns expected
C. How much wealth is needed to pay off all debt and have reasonable savings

The investment should be planned with a long term horizon from minimum 5 years to 10 years at the best or even more. Any short term planned returns may not be achieved if market conditions change due to economic and/or other geo political factors.

Targets should be set up depending on how many surplus funds are allocated for investment in stocks and projected wealth to be achieved over 5 to 10 years time. If you have less available funds, aggressive investments with reasonable caution should be planned. This has to be strictly monitored.

At appropriate time, it should be liquidated. Remember that we are not trying to time the market. It is almost impossible to time the market in always right direction. However once achieved what is needed, we may take some portion to liquidate and book profits and allow us to clean up portion of debts.

This exercise should be done periodically and reviewed to see if we are on targets. Again I reiterate that we cannot time the market 100% and never be 100% right. However stock market had never failed to go to new high over a period of time.

Follow the strategy with utmost discipline.

How much returns on investment are reasonable? This is very tricky question. Based on expected rate of returns, allocation of funds to aggressive, moderate and growth stocks should be done. If we cannot deploy funds in way that will generate higher returns than average returns of market, we should note that there is something wrong in our allocation, strategy etc.

Apart from that, all returns are compounding, meaning that it will generate more year after year. For example if you have planned to get 15% per annum on average, the wealth could be double in 5 years and that will go to quadruple in 10 years or less. The effect of this could be much higher if we can achieve average returns of 20% per annum. Check the math and see how amazing it can grow.

If the allocation of funds in to aggressive, moderate and growth are done properly and be changed according to market conditions periodically, we can surely achieve returns of over 20% per annum and this is done as per my experience.

Have faith, use funds allocation wisely; re plan strategy when needed. I have discussed this strategy and allocation separately showing wealth maximizer.

To summarize, we should set up our goals of getting percentage returns, allocation of funds and targets to achieve over span of 10 years and beyond.

Chapter: 3 Financial Conditions:

Stock market investment needs some surplus available savings. Whatever saving available, a person can start with. If started at an early age, it will give advantage of long innings, may be more than 20 years time.

So we should first of all, prepare a personal balance sheet which is summary of all personal assets and liabilities including all short term and long term. One will argue that to invest in stock market, why do we need a balance sheet?

Well, a balance sheet will give a complete health of personal financials and this will help you to decide the investment commitment, future goals and what strategy to adapt weather aggressive or moderate and growth. Remember the ultimate objective of investment is to have DEBT FREE living and have reasonable savings.

We should list down all assets and debts in these personal financial statements and then we can decide how much liquid cash available for investment in stock markets. This can be prepared joint of husband and wife.

Below is the format and after it is done, will discuss about the investment commitment in stock market

Personal Financial statement:

As of Date-_____

Assets	Amount
Cash in banks and on hand	
IRA or other retirement accounts	
Any notes receivable	

Stock and bond accounts	
Life Insurance cash value	
All real estate value	
All other assets including business Investment value (net)	
Total Assets	
Liabilities:	
Mortgage on real estate	
Any notes payable to bank/others	
All other liabilities	
Any accounts payable	
Total Liabilities	

Total Net Worth	
(All assets Less Total Liabilities)	

Notes:

A. Try to list out value of all assets and liabilities to the best possible value

B. Make a very reasonable efforts to decide on value

Now Identify available funds for investments:

Separate out cash and cash equivalent as per below:

	Amount
Cash in banks and on Hand	
IRA or other retirement accounts	
Stock and bond accounts	
Total funds available For investment:	

Here, if you already have investment in stock and bond accounts, it can be counted in stocks investments available because it can be reclassified or re arranged for our available funds. We may leave retirement accounts, as is for time being.

Now if the fund available in banks and existing stock account, for example is $ 500,000 then we need to decide how much one wants to commit for investments in stocks. You need to keep some cash in banks to meet the existing needs of current liabilities which is payments to be done within one year time including one year mortgage and other installments payments.

This factor will also be influenced by regular monthly income what we have as per below:

Monthly regular income:	Amount
Salary	
Other Investment income	
Any other monthly income	
Total Monthly Income	

Monthly payment liabilities:	
Monthly Installments	
Monthly home expenses	
Total Monthly expenses	

If monthly total income is more than monthly total expenses, then we are not for now, dependent on any stock market income. This will help us to decide with more comforts, our long term goals on investments and define objectives.

Now back to decision. If we have $500,000 in stock accounts and banks, we can commit anywhere from $250,000 to $400,000 after setting up our long term goals and desired wealth level. I would suggest we can go for 60 percent of above which is $300,000 and may be more.

Once the decision on funds to be invested is committed, and then strategy has to be decided as to go for aggressive, moderate and growth structure. Remember that we need to have long term wealth objective which best is 10 years and more. If we get 15% average annual returns, then in 10 years it will quadruple, from $ 300,000 to $ 1.2 million. Now look at your liability side of balance sheet. How much is your total liabilities.

Our goal is to have complete debt free living situation. Hence if total of all liabilities are, say $ 1.2 million, we can achieve this goals in 10 years at 15% average annual **compounding** returns. If liabilities are more than $ 1.2 million, we plan to commit funds into more aggressive structure fetching average annual returns higher, may be up to 20% per annum or have longer period of commitments like 15 years or so. Plus keep in mind that we need additional funds for retirement and other family needs which we need to consider.

Anything we decide, we must have faith and a plan, a complete strategy of allocation of suggested funds in different sectors, as discussed separately.

In this chapter, we are trying to find personal financial health and make a decision of how much investment funds we have available and what are our plans to achieve debt free living over a period of time. We need to find out available funds for investment in stocks and total liabilities to be paid off in future and how much funds we need for comfortable retirement saving.

Chapter 4: Profit & Loss-Personal:

Again, one would ask why we need to prepare profit & Loss for investment in stocks. Preparing profit & loss account periodically will give us an idea of how on track we are.

This is simple format of gains and losses in stocks can be prepared at the end of every 6 months. The plan is that, if we are not achieving what we want, it will allow us to do re adjustment in strategy. We should be flexible to adapt to changes when needed. Every investment strategy works in long run. We should give reasonable time to our planned works.

Let's see the simple format:

Profit & Loss account for period, Say Jan 1st 2017 to June 30 2017 (6 Months)

Total Gain/ Loss	Amount
A. **Gains**	
Realized in stocks during the period	
Unrealized gains as of end of period which is, Say June 30, 2017	
Total of A	
B. **Less Losses:**	
Losses realized in stocks during this period	
Unrealized loss as of June 30, 2017	
Total of B	
C: Total Gains/Loss in portfolio **(A less B)**	

Notes: 1. we can calculate gains realized from our brokers account of trades done during this 6 months period.

2. Similarly any loss realized will be also calculated from brokers account trades executed at loss.

3. For unrealized gains/loss, we need to put value of our portfolio as of end of June 30, 2017 and compare with what we have paid for those stocks. If amount paid is lower than current value, difference will be unrealized gain and if amount paid is more than current value, it will be unrealized loss.

Now let's go back to our original investment amount committed and invested in total portfolio. If for example, we have initially invested in stocks and cash balance, a total of $ 200,000 and our total gains as above, is say, $ 20,000 for the period, then our total gain is 20% annualized because we have prepared profit & Loss for 6 months only.

This percentage returns should be compared with what we have planned initially and sees that if we have achieved it or over/under achieved.

If we have achieved or over achieved, then we are doing well. But if our percentage return is lower than what we planned, we may need to do re adjustment in our portfolio. We must see what stocks not performing in our portfolio are, study them again and if needed, we may decide to sell it and go into different stocks in same/other sectors and leaders. I have discussed in this book separately, how to address this issue.

Remember, at the end of each period, I would suggest calculating this percentage returns on compounding basis. This will give wealth maximizer effect.

Chapter 5: Adjustments:

So, why do we need to adjust to our strategy?

Let us review the profit & loss account as discussed in the previous chapter.

First, go back to the goals set up earlier like say 15% or 20% compounding returns.

Second, check with our performance we have achieved in our prepared profit & loss.

If we have achieved or over achieved than what was set up, we are doing fine. Here we may continue what we have invested in. We may make some changes needed in sectors and individual stocks to have better results.

This is the process we should continue to do every 6 months and re evaluate the strategy.

Now, let us see if we have under achieved than the goals set. Let us say, if we had set up goals of 20% returns and we have achieved only 10%. Then we need to find out where we have gone wrong. We need to review our portfolio carefully and evaluate to see which stocks are not doing well. It may happen that some stocks may be doing well and some may not be.

We need to work on stocks not performing as per planned. First, we need to find out where we need to move our funds once we can sell nonperforming. We should be ready with list of shopping of estimated amount and also with identified stocks.

We should be ready to accept the fact that our decision was not correct on those nonperforming stocks. It is possible that out of these stocks, some may be good stocks but they are down may be for no reason. If they are in strong sector and nothing much wrong with fundamentals of the company, we may continue and give them second chance.

In short, when preparing a shopping list, we must keep in mind fundamentals and technicals of company as discussed in other chapter.

Most important thing, if some stocks are not performing, we should sell it and rearrange our portfolio so that we are back into game. We should be ready to do these adjustments. Once this adjustment is done, we also need to re set our planned goals of percentage returns on new adjusted investments.

We may not need to do any adjustments if the stocks are down due to economic/political factors and may continue. A rational decision is to be taken.

Chapter 6: Fearless Investment:

Before we decide to do investments in stocks, we must have faith in the system to generate sufficient wealth which will fulfill our goals set.

A confidence in system and self will help reduce the fear of loss. All investments should be planned with long term range of minimum 5 to 10 years and beyond. This will help us to ride ups and downs of economy and market conditions.

Once initial goals and targets are set for wealth to be achieved, we need to identify sectors and market leaders based on technicals and fundamentals as discussed in other chapters.

They need to be followed and the exercise should be done on continuous basis. We will be ready with the shopping list of companies and need to be watched for some time before jumping into it. Gradual investments will help reduce the fear. Remember that we may not be right always and according to my experience, the investment may not give desired results in short run.

Do not get frustrated. Have faith in companies based on fundamentals and technicals. Review them frequently and this will help reduce anxiety and fear. At various times, we need to identify leading sectors and companies under those sectors.

We have discussed this identification process in next chapters. Investment done with confidence and without fear will help reduce anxiety. Over a long run, stock market has never failed to go to new high. At frequent times, we need to adapt to change and we will do that which is adjustments.

The primary purpose to invest in stocks is to generate sufficient wealth and have debt free retirement with good amount of savings for self and family. Remember investment is following mass psychology ahead of time.

Chapter 7: Fundamentals and Technical's:

This is most important chapter leading us to identify companies where we need to invest. The process of identification requires study of fundamentals and technical's of companies.

Let us first discuss how to begin:

1. First of all we need to find out which are strong sectors.
2. Strong sectors can be technology, transportation, energy retail, banking etc. However I personally believe in TECHNOLOGY SECTOR which is most powerful amongst all time
3. After deciding on sectors, say, technology, we need to find out companies within that sector which we want to target to invest and then we

need to study them as per criteria listed here. Make a sorted list ready

4. We should not invest in more than 8 to 10 companies because it is hard to monitor them if more than 10 companies on continuous basis.

5. A simplified process to identify companies are POPULAR HOUSEHOLD NAMES and most used by YONGER generations.

On long run, companies with absolute cash balance are the best. Absolute cash balance means no short term or long term debt and cash per share is high.

What is cash per share? Total available cash and all liquid investments divided by number of shares outstanding. In today's technology world, we have lots of research web site where we can apply all technical's and fundamentals formulas to find a list of shares we wanted to invest. Use them.

Being a CPA, I am always a fan of companies having nearly no short or long term debts. There are multiples technicals and fundaments formats and formulas available. However we will discuss and apply only some as listed below. This will be more helpful and less confusing. As per my experience this is most effective in achieving our goals.

I have been using **Finviz.com** to do my research and you can use similar other companies on subscription basis.

Let us discuss below most important fundamentals and technical's ratios and research we use. Each one is described in simple way. Remember all this formula values are instantly available on various stocks research web site. The explanation is for knowledge why we are using them.

1. **Book/share**. This is book value of the company per one share. Total net asset of the company divided by total outstanding shares.

2. **Cash/share**. Cash per available share is total cash available with the company including all liquid cash and all cash equivalents divided by total outstanding number of shares.
   Higher cash per share is better because company can withstand all economic downturn situations in future.

3. **Debt/Equity**. Total debt of the company, all types, divided by total outstanding number of shares. The best companies are with zero debt. I personally go with company having no debt.

4. **LT debt/Equity**. Total long term debt of the company divided by total outstanding number of shares. Again, the best companies are with zero debt. I personally go with company having no debt.
5. **EPS.** Earnings per share are total earnings made by company divided by total outstanding number of shares. This can be per each quarter. We need to see if EPS are going up or down compared to each quarters.
6. **Inst. Own**: Institutional ownership percentage. This is total percentage shares owned by financial institution in the company. Higher the percentage, more confidence in the company by institution. We want to see gradual increase in percentage of institution holding in the company.

7. **Insider own**. If the insider/owners of the company hold higher percentage of total shares, it may be better sign that the owners have bigger stake in the company.

8. **Target price**. This is average of all separate target price set by analyst following the company. Target price is important as to see what price we are buying the share and what is price targeted to have by analysts.

9. **RSI (14):** Relative strength index. RSI is measured for 14 days. If the share is relatively strong and this can range from index 10 to 90. RSI 90 is very high and it could be selling. Contrary RSI under 20 is mostly a buy because it is oversold. However this should be looked along with all other formulas as discussed.

10. **52 week high/low**: This is the range of share traded in last 52 weeks. What is high within last 52 weeks and what is lowest price within last 52 weeks.

The important point, we cannot do individual research as above on thousands of listed companies. We need to have some basic formulas where we can target and find out companies. I have not given too many formulas here. We can take rational decision on simplified way.

First, a decision as to, what sectors to choose which is likes technology, banking, transportation etc.

Second, is percentage allocation of our potential investment which I have suggested somewhere else in this book. How much percentage we need to allot to different companies and how much cash we should have it.

Thirdly, list of companies identified for our review; apply all parameters and short list on watch list.

Then be ready to invest as per our allocation.

In order to make the process simple, I have discussed the allocation, identification of company's process as per our goals in next chapter. This will help and make it a simple process.

Apart from all above formula, HISTORICAL VOLUME, daily range of the share which is days open, days high and days low with closing price of individual share is equally important.

Once all above listed formulas were applied to make a list of companies ready, we should find out historical price/volume data. I personally use **yahoo/finance** here. You can get historical data on yahoo/finance or any other related web site. Put the symbol of company and go in to historical pricing. Here last 20 days pricing is more important.

Check closing price of stock on each last 20 days. If the price of stock is closing higher than previous with higher volume than previous, it means more people are buying it. If it is lower on lower volume, it may be ok. Remember, all stocks cannot just go up and up every day. It could go down on down day or any day. However if the volume is lower on down side than previous days, the rising trend is still there.

Have faith in self. Follow the steps. I am not too big fan of charting. However a stock chart can be used for 6 months period, a simple chart to see it does have higher highs and lower lows. A trend line can be drawn to see if stock is going high. A simple thing to see in chart is to see higher highs and lower lows.

In longer range more important factors are:

1. All above formulas applied to find out strong fundaments of the company. Strong healthy company.
2. Historical volume data to see the trend is intact.
3. A simple chart to see higher highs and lower lows.

Remember we are making investment keeping a long term horizon and it is not done based on day trading formula. If the investment is done in stronger company for long term, it will give you desired results.

Again, stock market has never failed to go to new high over a period of time.

Just not to get confused as how to find good companies, use popular household daily use names and technology used by younger generations, like **apple, face book, goggle, Amazon,** etc. Make a complete list of those about 25 to 30 companies. Then apply above formulas to short list 12 to 15 companies. Watch them, follow the system and formulas as above and we will be ready to invest.

Chapter 8: Identified Lists:

Identification of companies targeted to invest is crucial and critical. I have tried to make this process simple and effective based on my investment experience. But this requires some work here. Because we are making investment in individual stocks rather than index. Investment in index moves along with markets ups and downs. However it is possible that investment in companies can move ups and downs depending on news, strength and market conditions

First, let us list our basic criteria:

1. We decided to invest in individual stocks and again, not more than 10 companies at a time. Because we wanted to monitor, follow up closely.

We should know internal health of the company first and then market and economic conditions

2. NEVER USE MARGIN borrowing. Whatever best cash available is our deployable investment. I am surely against margin borrowing because it may wipe us out and then over a period of time, the stocks may go up and we keep watching and regretting. Our basic philosophy is to achieve debt free life and have strong solid savings for family. Investment is an art and not a gambling and should not bring anxiety.

3. Decide and write down sectors in which we want to invest. Technology, biotech, finance etc. I prefer to go in few sectors at a time. Technology is the best. In present era, there are always changing technology and companies moving at a rapid speed with upcoming technology.

Remember this book is to guide to maximize the investment returns and hence I have adapted aggressive approach.

4. Have faith in self. Investments are mass psychology and we have to follow it correctly ahead of most of people. So stay with the approach and do not keep changing frequently. However, if we are wrong constantly, we should be ready to adapt change, get rid of losing battle and move on. It may happen that initially, once investment is done, it may not give desired results instantly. But investment done with long term objective and if stayed with our steps, it will give desired results, may be even more.

5. Now very important is allocation of funds available. We need to plan how much percentage of available funds to

invest where etc. My percentage formula is suggested below:

A. Invest up to 60% of funds in moderate aggressive portfolio. Here only good companies are selected and it could be only 6 to 7 companies under this **plan A**. I am not in favor of heavy diversification of portfolio

B. Invest up to 20% of funds available in aggressive and fast moving companies based on STRONG BALANCE SHEET. Here note that I am putting emphasis on balance sheet and not profit and loss. If balance sheet is strong along with good plans and management, company can come up and give us huge returns in future. Investment made under this formula may give us 50 percent and more returns. I personally suggest having 3 to 4 companies only under this **plan B**.

C. Balance of 20% or little more, always keep in cash available. This is very important to have some cash available. It can be used when there is extreme fall in market to average it out. Again, stock market has never failed to go to new high. The investment done with this additional cash can bring us additional returns. Follow the formula of LIFO which is last in first out. So whatever invested out of this 20 percent can be sold first with profits in future to bring back cash level.

D. The investment in A and B above should be done gradually and in small quantity. For example, if 10 percent of funds are targeted to invest in company like Apple under plan A above, 5 percent can be done at one time, another 5 percent can be deployed after some time when comfortable. This way it can be averaged out. The reason we follow this is that we presume we are never always right. Averaging out is best way to ride the wave. And similar pattern should be followed in plan B above in aggressive investment.

E. So all together we will have 10 companies invested in and it can be watched, followed up more diligently.

Now, after setting up percentage allocation and formulas as above, more important question is as to how to identify investment in those 10 companies.

Based on my experience, I have suggested below process to follow:

1. First investment in plan A companies which is major portion of our investment up to 60 percent. Going back to chapter Fundamentals and Technicals. Once a decision is made to choose sectors, say technology, banking etc we need to find good companies with market leaders. I personally would stick more towards technology companies. There is good web site available to apply formulas to find companies. I have been using Finviz.com and yahoo/finance. The strongest companies are always in lime light. Like **aapl, amzn, baba, goog, fb, tsla, msft, nflx** etc. These leaders can always be rotating and changes may happen during different time period. However some of them are always leaders.

2. So above are general leaders we can list out under watch list. To add on more, we can find another strong sector which could be banking, transportation etc and add to the list market leaders in those sectors. It is so easy to find our leaders because they are household names and talked about. Having listed all good companies may be list of 25 or so companies; we can apply some formulas as discussed in chapter 7. Go to Finviz.com and yahoo/finance. We can check each and every identified companies book/share, cash/share, debt/equity, EPS etc. Check all 10 parameters as listed. Write in note pad for all these companies we have decided to review. I will further screen out companies with growing EPS, intuitional ownership and most important cash per share and

debt/equity. I personally prefer company with very low debt/equity or zero borrowing and high cash per share with growing EPS. If the company's earnings are growing with nearly zero debt, those stocks are always favored by mass and it will continue to go up. This process will help us to have target list reduce from 25 stocks to may be 10 to 12 stocks.

3. Put these 12 stocks under our daily watch list. Observe their price movement for some time. Apply historical price/volume from yahoo/finance or any other web site to see if volume is going up when price goes up. Compare for last 20 days and continue this on daily basis. Now we are ready to invest out of these 12 stocks. To simplify, I suggest to have low debt or no debt, growing EPS, higher cash

per share, little lower RSI say RSI of 45 or low and historical price/volume (higher high on higher volume than previous volume). This is applicable to market and sector leaders only like **aapl, amzn, goog** etc. This is little bit safe investment but can give us average annual returns of 10 to 15 percent and 60 percent of our portfolio is in these good stocks, 6 to 7 companies. We keep lower number because we can watch; monitor and see that they perform as required and if not can be changed. Remember, all investments are done on long term basis and hence small amount of time can be given to see their movement on mostly daily basis.

4. If we have allotted 10 percent of available funds to company like AAPL, we may start with half of it immediately and balance remaining we can deploy

after a small period of time. This may help us to average it out or give a chance to review more carefully. Gradually we will reach 6 to 7 companies with 60 percent. But should be done in reasonable time. Have faith and do it.

5. Is above too confusing? Just list out general household names and we use it on daily basis, names of companies like **apple, face book, Google, Netflix, Bank of America, etc.** Simply make a list of those companies especially more frequently used by younger generations which could be Apple, Face Book, Amazon, Google and we use them on daily routine. If we have those popular 25 companies ready, then apply 10 formulas as listed in previous chapter, we will be ready to invest in 6/10 companies.

under **plan A**. This is most effective and simple approach.

Investment under **plan B:**

1. This is my favorite investment of 20 percent portfolio or little higher. Reason, it can give up to 100 percent return or may be more. The selection process is again simple. This is BALANCE SHEET INVESTMENT. I would focus more here on cash per share and debt/equity, long term debt/equity, RSI parameters of the company. Let me give some example. Some biotech companies sometimes fall to 70 to 90 percent in price on some news of failed drugs etc. The price per share goes down to half or even more than available cash per share. More important to see that if company has no debt at all or nearly no long/short term

debt and what is cash burn rate. Let's say if they have $ 2 cash per share and cash burn rate per quarter is 22 cents, then safely this company can remain in business for next 8 quarters and do their research in another drugs etc. We need the stock price to watch for some days before deciding to invest. RSI may have fallen under 20 which are typically oversold. Similar situation may have been occurred in any other stock in any sector, the reason may be lower earnings than anticipated etc. Note that the lower price trading should not be result of fraudulent management, bankruptcy filing etc. But a normal business reason like failed drug trial, lower earning than anticipated etc. This can happen in any sector including technology, bio tech. and stock is trading at ridiculously low bargain.

Make a separate watch list of this type of stocks with low RSI, higher cash per share and nearly zero debt. Key is that the company should not go bankrupt in less than 2 years and judgment can be taken from cash burn rate. Cash burn rate can be seen from their previous quarter earning generally available on stock analysis web site like finviz.com.

2. After identifying those falling companies we need to find out an angel to invest. Remember we have to invest in 4 to maximum 5 stocks here. Do not want uncontrollable investment.

3. Continue to watch these fallen angels. Update list. You can find them from top looser list daily. We can put them on our watch list and then apply the parameters as discussed above. Note that we need debt free company with high cash per share and low RSI. This

indicates a better balance sheet price than the current trading price. Looks a bargain. However this bargain needs to be combined with other aspect such as cash burn rate, trading volume, RSI. On your watch list here, after some time, trading volume will go to really low like normal or less than normal average. This is the time to step in and buy. If we have 5 percent funds available to invest in one company, we can start with half of it first. Watch it for some time may be like few weeks. Then invest balance of half. Sometimes it may happen that our half invested may start giving some good results before we apply another half. We may then decide not to invest remaining but enjoy the fruits of higher trading price. Again, we are doing long term investment. Over and after some time, the bargain stocks do attract other investors and they jump into it. It may happen that after one or two quarters company may come out with new product, change in management, effective cost cutting etc.

4. If proper time is given on these 20 percent portfolio, it may give us 100 percent or more returns. We may Sell them once we achieve 50 percent and above returns and move on with other stocks. This portfolio is on continuous watch. If a particular stock is not moving within 3 to 6 months time, we may sell it and move on with other stock. Continue this process and based on my experience, it had given more than 100 percent annual returns. However we cannot deploy more than certain percentage in this type and hence I suggested 20 percent of

portfolio to maximum 25 percent with 4 to 5 companies only at a time.

The remaining cash balance of 20 percent or little more can be used only in certain time. Note that no margin at all. Keep cash available of 20 percent minimum. A time will come when there is severe drop in market including our invested stocks under **plan A** of good companies. During this time we may use part of this cash balance to invest in our good companies , add some more may be 10 percent of available cash funds in each good one and when market stabilize and goes up, sell these additional bought under **LIFO**, last in first out. Bring back cash level to minimum 20 percent. Market will go up over a period of time and at that time good leaders will also go higher. We don't need to average out aggressive stocks invested under **plan B**.

I have given a simplified spreadsheet chart of all above in last chapter. But a basic understanding and study is required as discussed. If proper deployment of funds is done as discussed, it may give us average annual returns above 20 percent. This can go up really fast when we calculate and achieve cumulative returns. The portfolio value can be doubled in 4 years or less and see the compounding math in 10 years. This can help you to achieve debt free living over a period of time. Earlier we start investment, sooner we can achieve this.

Chapter 9: Investment:

Now time to invest. After following chapter 8, we must be ready with our list under **plan A** to deploy 60 percent and under **plan B** to deploy 20 percent.

1. The first list is a watch list under plan A of 12 to 15 companies as screened out. Here we have invested 60 percent of our available balance in maximum 6 to 7 companies. Watch them for some days. Apply volume based historical price approach of last 20 days of higher volume than previous one with high in price. This shows accumulation. Along with this, high cash per share, low or zero debt company and growing EPS will be preferred.

2. Invest at first place half of investment balance allocated. For example, if 10

percent of total funds are allocated to a company AAPL, invest half of it first and watch it for some days and then deploy balance of half. Follow this and deploy full 60 percent in 6 to 7 companies

3. Similarly, we should have second watch list ready under plan B to deploy 20 percent of available balance. This is crucial list of companies fallen in price. We need to make a list of companies as per procedure discussed in chapter 7and 8, fallen angels. Review higher cash per share than current trading price, no debt at all or very low debt, cash burn rate to survive for 2 years or more. Continue to watch them till selling volume cools down. This can be seen from comparable historical price/volume date of last 20 days. We may use yahoo/finance or any other source data.

4. Again start with half of decided investment first, for example, if we plan to invest 5 percent of available funds, we use half of it first to buy. Watch them for some time. It may happen that it may start going really high in few days. Then we may enjoy the ride and stay away with balance of half. Otherwise we can use remaining half of allocated funds and buy more. We need to have 4 to 5 companies only so that can monitor closely and take decisions when needed.

5. Note that purpose of investment is to have **debt free living** in the long term and not a day trading. I believe, reasonable wealth can be created over a period of time. Taking in to account 20% or more average annual returns when compounded, the investment can be doubled in 4 years or less and

quadruple in 8 years or less. The math is amazing. If long term planning is made, we can give sufficient time to ride negative economic, political and other factors.

6. The remaining 20 percent cash balance should be kept available and should be used only in severe sell off time as discussed in chapter 8. At a time of severe sell off, may be due to economic or political situation, we should have patience and self confidence and no fear. Market will eventually go up when dust settles down. However during this time, we may use these available cash to average out in **plan A** companies only in small quantity. When market is back up again, we can sell these additional purchase under **LIFO** (last in first out) and bring back our cash level to 20 percent or more.

I have tried to follow simple method of identifying companies under **plan A** and **plan B** investments. Plan A companies are **popular** daily use **household names** and products used by **younger generations**. This is simple method of making list of 25 companies under our watch list and applies formulas. Plan B is very aggressive **balance sheet investment**. But it can give us more than 50 percent returns and our average annual returns of whole portfolio could be 20 percent or higher and based on compounding portfolio over a period of time, we can achieve our goals of debt free living and reasonable savings.

I have purposely **used repetition** of formulas and methods so that after reading this book, the investment decision becomes mechanical process.

Chapter 10: Follow Up:

Follow up of our investment is required to see if we are doing right. The review should be done mostly on daily basis.

1. Note that we have to watch 10 invested stocks in total companies invested. The reason we kept number low so that we can monitor them closely, check related news, announcement etc. Plus we can check historical volume/price movement daily to see if the stock is making higher highs, lower lows.

2. We do have SECOND WATCH LIST ready other than above which is called TARGET LIST for changes or additional investment. These includes both for future planned investment under **plan A** and **plan B** type of companies. This list will be updated based on formulas

discussed in chapter 7 and relative bargains happened in different companies.

3. It is required to constantly monitor what we have invested in. It is possible that we may not have made correct decision in few stocks which are not performing. And we should be in a position to take a decision as to sell those non performing stocks and replace it from other list ready under watch list.

4. A sufficient reasonable time should be given to our invested stocks to perform. Remember that our philosophy is not a day trading. Key decision is when to sell a non performing stock or change in to relative bargain.

First let us discuss about non performing stock situation.

A. We have investment made under plan A and plan B. Plan A investment is done in 6 to 7 really good companies which comprises about 60 percent of our total funds. For example investments in companies like **aapl, fb, amzn, goog, baba** etc. Example is given for guidance only at this time. Out of above if a particular company is not doing well in stock pricing, we have to sell it and replace with another company. Our 1 year price target growth is minimum 10 percent annualized. If we bought the stock at say for $ 100 and after 6 months if the price is above $ 105, then annualized rate of return is 10 percent. But again, this decision should be taken after considering overall market conditions. We can continue to hold lower performing stock if negative market conditions are there or price/volume historical data do not suggest selling. Selling of stock decision should not be taken too frequently as we are not a day trader.

B. Investment made under **plan B,** 4 to 5 aggressive stocks, they should be reviewed periodically. We need to give sufficient time here as these stocks are way down, sold off. It may take some time till some good news from management etc come and being accumulated by institutions, investors, based on balance sheet investment. My experience suggests that it will happen over little longer period sometimes say 6 months. But when it happens, they move **parabolic** and may go up by 100 percent or even more. Here even if we are correct in only 2 stocks, it can give us bumper rate of returns. Our personal targeted returns are almost 50 percent per annum on average. However we cannot invest more than 20 percent of funds as this is bit riskier and investment is an art.

Bargain swap is equally very important decision. What is bargain swap? This is crucial judgment decision. For example, we may have invested in **aapl** and **fb** and their prices are almost similar. At some point of time, due to temporary adverse news, like **aapl** may have extreme selling pressure and it goes down more than usual. This may become bargain, for example; price of **aapl** is lower more by 10 to 15 percent than **fb**. Let me give dollar example. **Aapl** and **fb,** in similar group trading at $ 150 each. If **aapl** is sold off heavier and price goes down to $ 135 or lower, then it is relative bargain as compared to **fb** at that time trading at $150. If we have **fb** 100 shares, then we can sell and buy 110 **aapl**, may be add more in our existing portfolio or out of watch list. Over a period of time, when they are back to near same price, we can sell **aapl** and buy **fb**. This way we are back into the same stock but higher quantity of 110 shares. This requires skilled judgment decision and should be done only within similar group type of shares. Sooner or later it happens provided there is no permanent negative news like failed product, drop in earnings etc. The drop in price should be temporary mass psychological sell off.

Bargain swap should be done very carefully and mostly be done under invested **plan A** stocks. We may get similar bargain situation in invested group plan B. We can take an extremely careful decision here to go into bargain swap. If a real strong bargain based on balance sheet, cash per share, volume/price analysis happens, only then we consider. This should not be done too frequently. But situation may come and we can take an advantage of it. **The goal is to increase number of shares without additional investment and get back into the same share again.**

Never sell everything. We must have faith in self and market and have to sail in the boat whether it is smooth sailing or titanic sailing. Opportunity do come during titanic sailing and at that time apply bargain swap strategy and/or additional cash available out of 20 percent.

Also winning and performing position, do not sell. Continue investment for longer term. We may never have to sell few good stocks under **plan A** and continue to enjoy the growth in price and portfolio value.

I have discussed all general points and defense mechanism in different chapter.

Chapter 11: Goals:

1. Goals need to be set up before we start investing. This is important because we need to see and compare if we are doing as per targets and plans.

2. Effort should be made to have reasonable goals and targets. If we set up extremely high goals, it may not be achieved and leads to disappointment.

3. Before setting up goals, we should analyze our personal balance sheet, financial situation. How much debt we have including all personal long term, home loans and all other type of debts. For example if we have total debts put together, say $ 1.2 million then we need to add on here how much we need to have for comfortable retirement savings. So total debt of $1.2 million

plus targeted additional retirement savings, say, another $1.3 million. Our combined goals are set to have now $2.5 million, total to be achieved.

4. Now key is that how many liquid funds we have available for investment in stocks and number of years target investment to achieve debt free living with reasonable retirement savings. If we start this at early younger age, we could give long term horizon. But most important is available funds for investment. I am personally against borrowing money and do investments. Whatever best available funds, we start with that.

5. With a combined investment as suggested in plan A stocks and plan B stocks, I would set up average annual returns of 18 to 20 percent. Now compounding math is amazing. Our

investment will be **doubled** in 4 years and **quadruple** in 8 years and it can grow up to 8 times in 12 years. Given some error in time calculation, we can safely say it can grow 8 times in 14 years and 15 times of original investment in 20 years. This is very safe and conservative calculation. If things move really as planned, it can go up to 20 times in 20 years or even more.

6. Back to our total target of achieving $2.5 million as per Para 3 above. If we target to achieve 20 times in 20 years, a total of $2.5 million, then we need to start with $125,000 initial investment. With this initial investment of $125,000, we will be achieving our goal of $2.5 million in 20 years at the rate of 20 times and have paid off all debts and have retirement savings.

7. Above calculation can be redefined based on our requirement of targets to be achieved and number of years available. Again, we do plan long term strategy and this is not for really short term and day trading. The suggested permutation should be done carefully and within achievable. I personally suggest, based on my experience, 18 to 20 percent annualized returns are achievable. So calculate the math accordingly.

I have given this chapter nearly at the **end of book** because before setting up the goals, we need to make full balance sheet/personal financials and understand concept of investment and formulas, to see where we stand and what we need to achieve so that a proper planning can be made.

Chapter 12: New Balance Sheet:

Why do we need to prepare our balance sheet at the end of every year? This is balance sheet of personal assets and liabilities.

Main reason to prepare it at the end of every year, is to compare how we are doing? Are we on track as per our goals? Assets side of the balance sheet should be getting stronger every year.

I have given again format which is now **comparables** as to the previous year.

Personal Financial statement:

As of Date-_____

Assets	Amount	Amount

	Beginning of Year	End of Year
Cash in banks and on Hand		
IRA or other retirement accounts		
Any notes receivable		
Stocks and bonds accounts		
Life Insurance cash value		
All real estate value		
All other assets including business Investment value (net)		
Total assets		
Liabilities:		
Mortgage on real estate		

Any notes payable to bank/others		
All other liabilities		
Any accounts payable		
Total liabilities		
Total net worth		
(All assets Less Total Liabilities)		

Notes:

1. The above Balance sheet/Personal financial statement is now comparables as to the beginning of the year.
2. We should prepare it once a year, mostly at the end of each year. The beginning year balances will be the ending balance of the previous year except for the first year.

3. If we check the comparable amount of beginning and end of the year balances, we should see the improvement in asset side, mainly the ending balance, and our investment in stocks and as a result of this our total net worth will be more at the end of the year as compared to beginning of the year.

4. If we have set our goals and targets of 20 percent average annual returns, we will be in a position to see as how much investment in stock account has changed at the end of year. Is it 20 percent or more? Let us check and see and this will help us to decide if we are doing right.

5. If there are not substantial improvements in the ending balance of our stock investments, we need to re plan the strategy and find out which stocks are not performing, both under

plan **A** and **plan B** investments. Non performing stocks, we may change to other better one from our target list of other stocks. Again we need to study here for the stocks to change as discussed in this book based on fundamentals and technicals.

6. It is possible that we may not need to change any stocks. We may continue based on technicals and other economic situation. However the decision has to base on as per formulas and methods discussed in this book earlier.

Chapter 13: Defense Mechanism:

Keep in mind following general points and follow them which can help to achieve our goals:

1. **NEVER SELL EVERYTHING** what we have invested in. Because we presume that we are never always right and no one will be. We have to sail in to the boat weather it is smooth sailing or titanic sailing. Market will eventually recover and go up. History tells that stock market has never failed to go to new high in long run.

2. During an economic slowdown time, we should review and attempt to make a **BARGAIN SWAP** as discussed in this book. And we may deploy additional cash balance we have, as per formula discussed in this book and sell this

additional shares on **LIFO(last in first out)**

3. **Continue invested**. Winning position in shares, do not sell it. They are winners because they are wanted by mass people. We don't have to sell really good and stable shares. We may not get chance to re enter back.

4. **HAVE FAITH** in self and market. If comparable balance sheet at the end of the years tells that we have achieved our target, then better enjoy the fruits rather than doing experiments.

5. Our goal is **long term investments** and strategy. The book is not for day trading. Follow fundamentals and technical's of the stock more as discussed. Sometimes chart of the stock can be deceptive. But if fundamentals and technical's are strong, then stock

will come back in future. We are not trying to time the market and stock.

6. Winning investment strategy is following **mass people's** psychology and when the whole group of people follows it, it becomes winning situation. We need to find out stocks and invest there before the whole mass jumps into it.

7. For any reason, if we are wrong in our investment in any particular stock, we should review it again, its fundamentals and technical's. And if we decide to change it, we should do it. **Our ego** should not come in the way thinking that why we are wrong?

8. At some point of time, heavy sell off may happen in all stocks due to economic and/or political situation. Stay calm during that time. May be stay away from market, give time to the

market to stabilize and then use available additional cash to average out in small quantity. We are not trying to time the market but following rules of **AVERAGING** in good stocks.

Chapter 14: Final Summary:

The following is the summary of investments decision in stocks. The chart is shown to simplify what we have discussed in previous chapters. This may be printed or written in own notepad so that the formulas are **ALWAYS AVAILABLE** to follow. I have presumed available funds to be invested at $ 200,000.

% of funds Allotted	Investment Decision	Formulas
60 percent of Available fund- $ 120,000	Total 6 to 7 good company's only under **plan A** Investments	Apply/Follow formulas as per chapter 7.Popular Household names.
20 percent	Total 4 to 5	Apply/Follow

of Available fund -$ 40,000	Fallen angels company under **plan B** balance sheet Investment	formulas as per chapter 7
20 percent of Available fund- $ 40,000	Cash balance to be used only when necessary to Average out and sell Per **LIFO**	Use of cash only when market falls to extreme as discussed in other chapters

Notes:

1. The above format should be used for all investment decision under **plan A** and **Plan B**.
2. Under Plan A, maximum number of companies should be 6 to 7 only and not more than 10 percent of total funds should be invested in EACH company. We should start with half

of the funds first and balance half be used after some time in same company.

3. Plan A target company list is simple. Most **POPULAR HOUSEHOLD** names and more frequently used by **younger generations** like **apple, face book, Google etc**. Apply formulas to this list and make decision. Mostly, I prefer cash rich and debt free companies with growing earnings.

4. Under plan B, maximum number of companies to be invested may be 4 only. Not more than 5 percent of total funds should be invested in **EACH** of that company. Follow the same method as per above.

5. Balance of 20 percent should be kept as cash available. This available cash can be used only under distress **market selloff**. Remember market

will come back over period of time and it will go to new high. Hence use this 20 percent to average out in plan A companies only and sell this additional investment on **LIFO(last in first out)** when market goes up and bring back cash level.

6. We should have **2 watch lists** of companies ready for investments. Watch list number 1 for target investment under plan A and B and watch list number 2 for future changes and additional investments. This should be updates frequently.

7. When a particular stock is not performing as planned, we should be ready to change it. Give it a reasonable time based on market conditions and then take decision as explained in other chapters.

8. **Have faith** in self and follow the mass psychology ahead of time.
9. Relative **BARGAIN** and **SWAP** method may be used as explained in previous chapters. This is VERY important decision. If done properly and should be done to increase quantity of good share under plan A investment as discussed in previous chapter.
10. Set up goals should be reviewed at end of the year by making comparable balance sheet/personal financial statement. This is required to see that we are achieving what we planned to have **DEBT FREE** life over long term with good reasonable savings.
11. Frequently review our investments and always monitor it. This will help us to make proper decision and achieve our goals.

12. Make a short list of **technical's and fundamental** formulas to apply to stocks we have to invest in. This ready list will help to memorize and become routine application in decision process.

13. You may find some statements and formats, uses of phrase etc **repetitive** and they are being done with purpose. Once you read the book completely, the system will set in mind and one will be able to **follow the system mechanically**. Hence repetition is done with this reason.

   Print this last chapter and memorize it.

I hope my personal experience thru this book may help you to achieve your goals of debt free living and wishing you best of luck. For any questions/clarification, you may email me at vrajeshchokshi@yahoo.com

VRAJESH CHOKSHI, CPA

www.ingramcontent.com/pod-product-compliance
Lightning Source LLC
Chambersburg PA
CBHW070407220526
45467CB00001B/501